Creative Mandalas 2

Mandala Coloring Books Vol.2

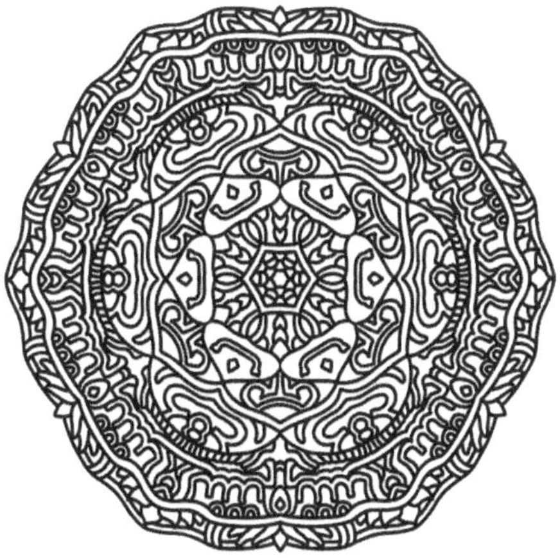
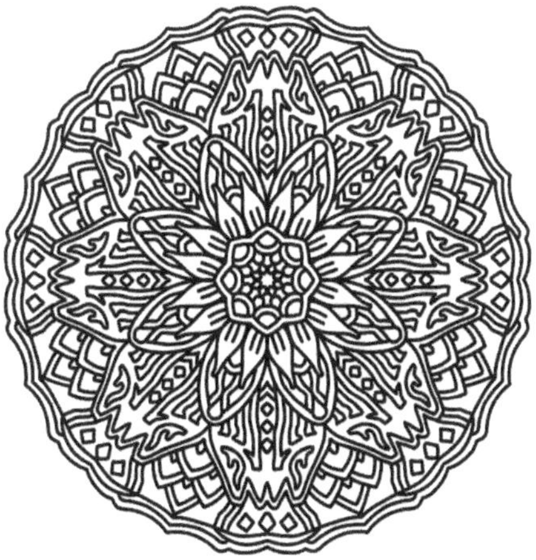
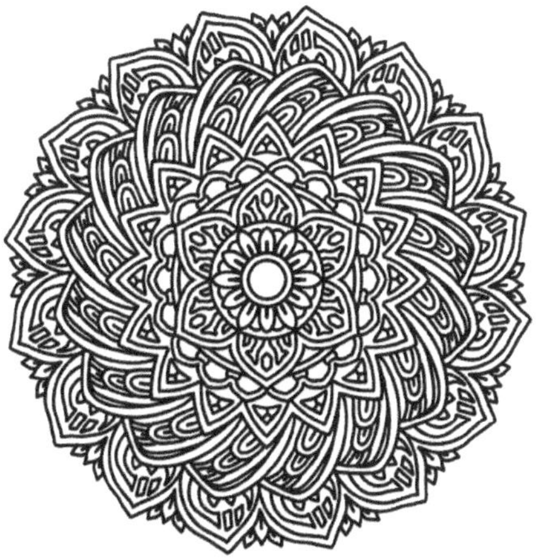

Karim Benyagoub

ISBN-10: 1514197456

ISBN-13: 978-1514197455

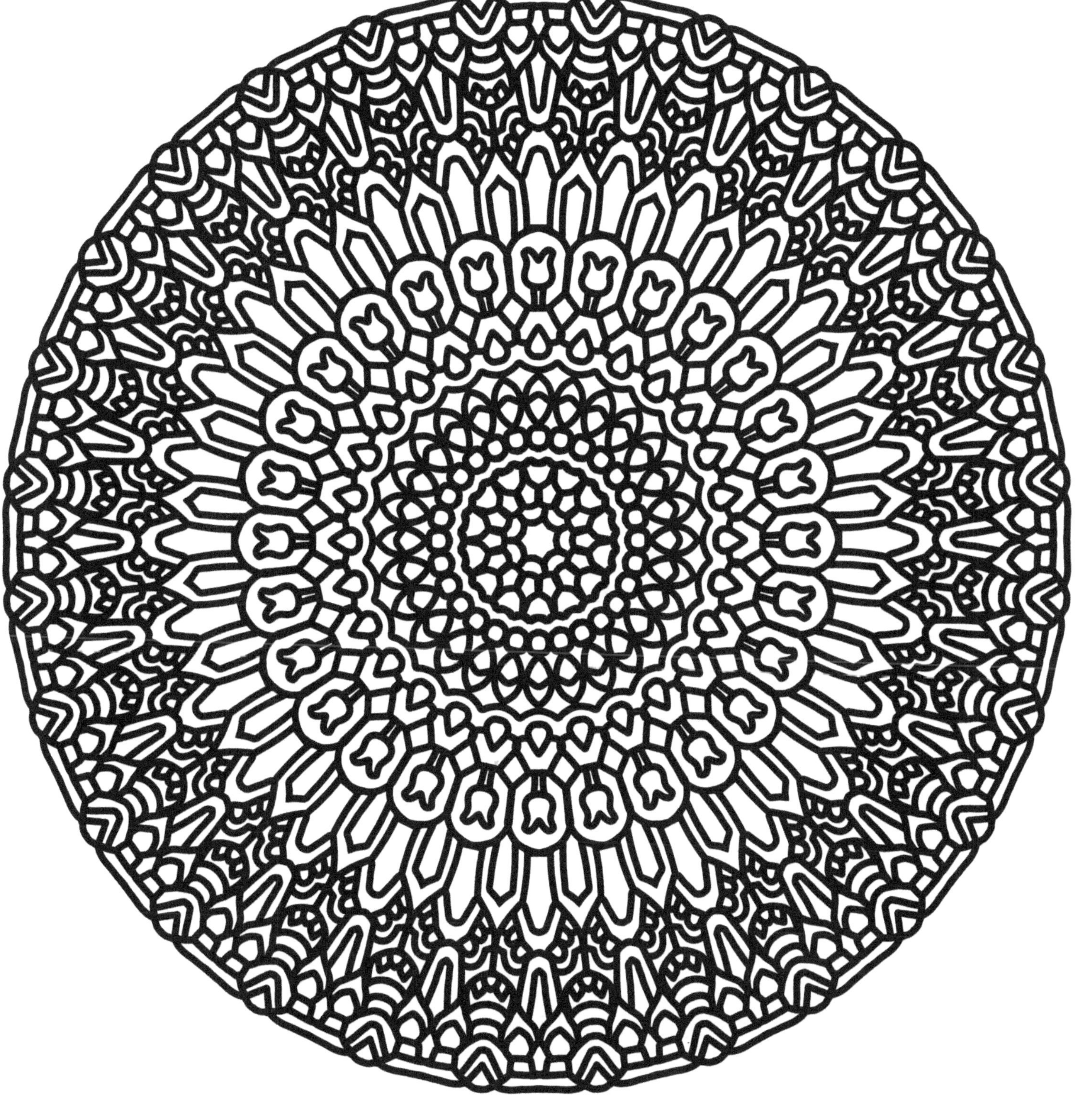

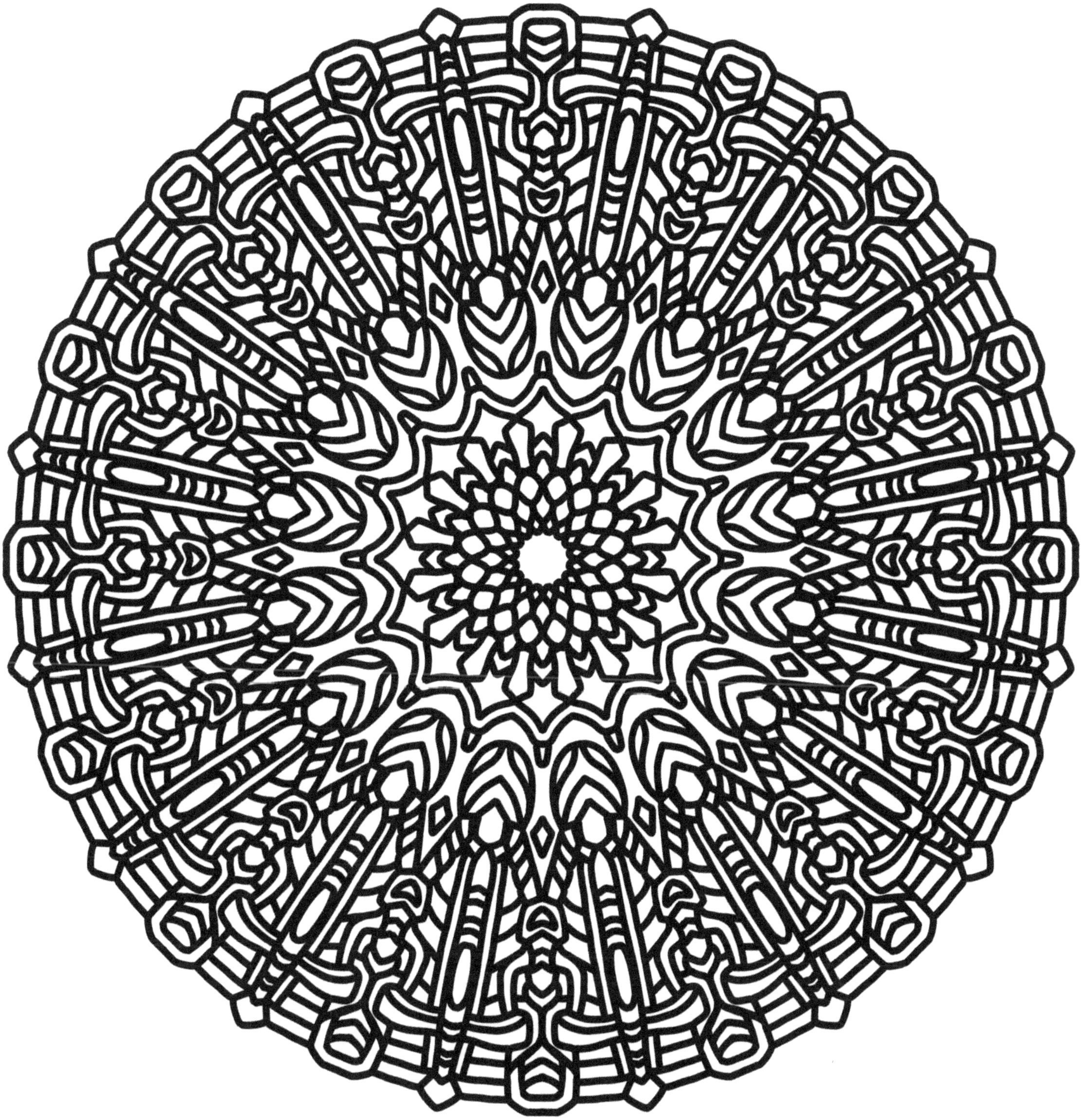

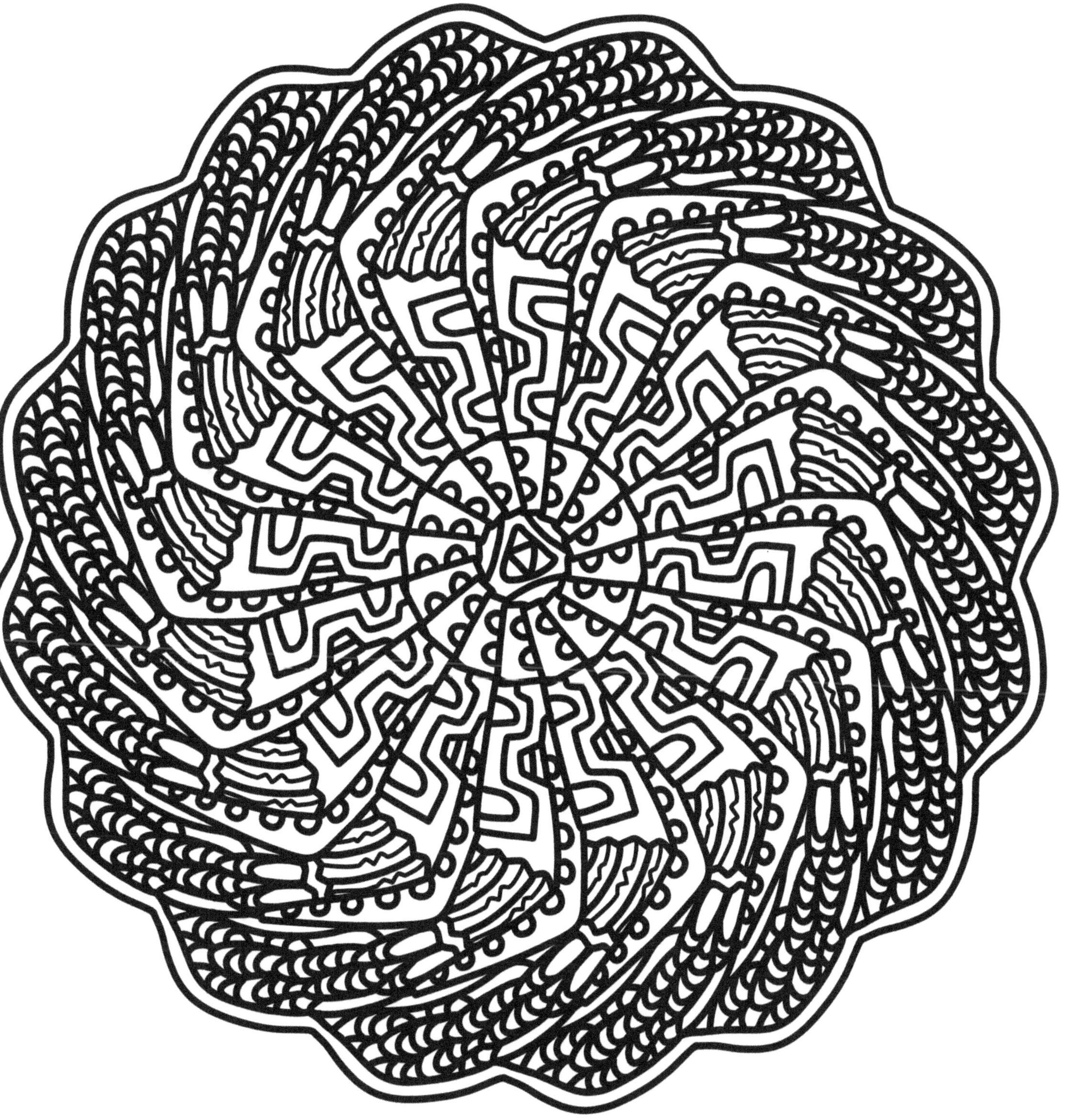

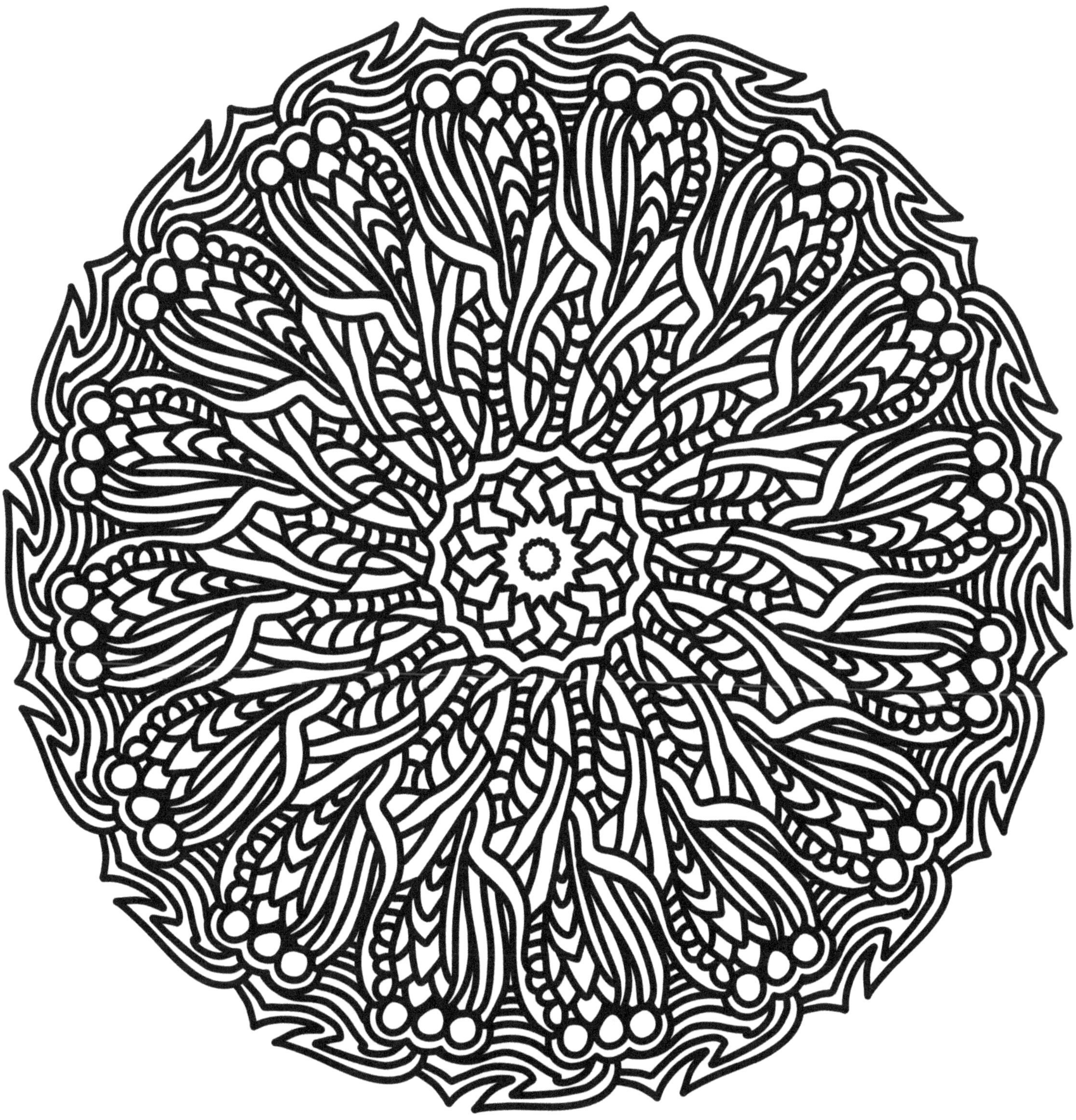

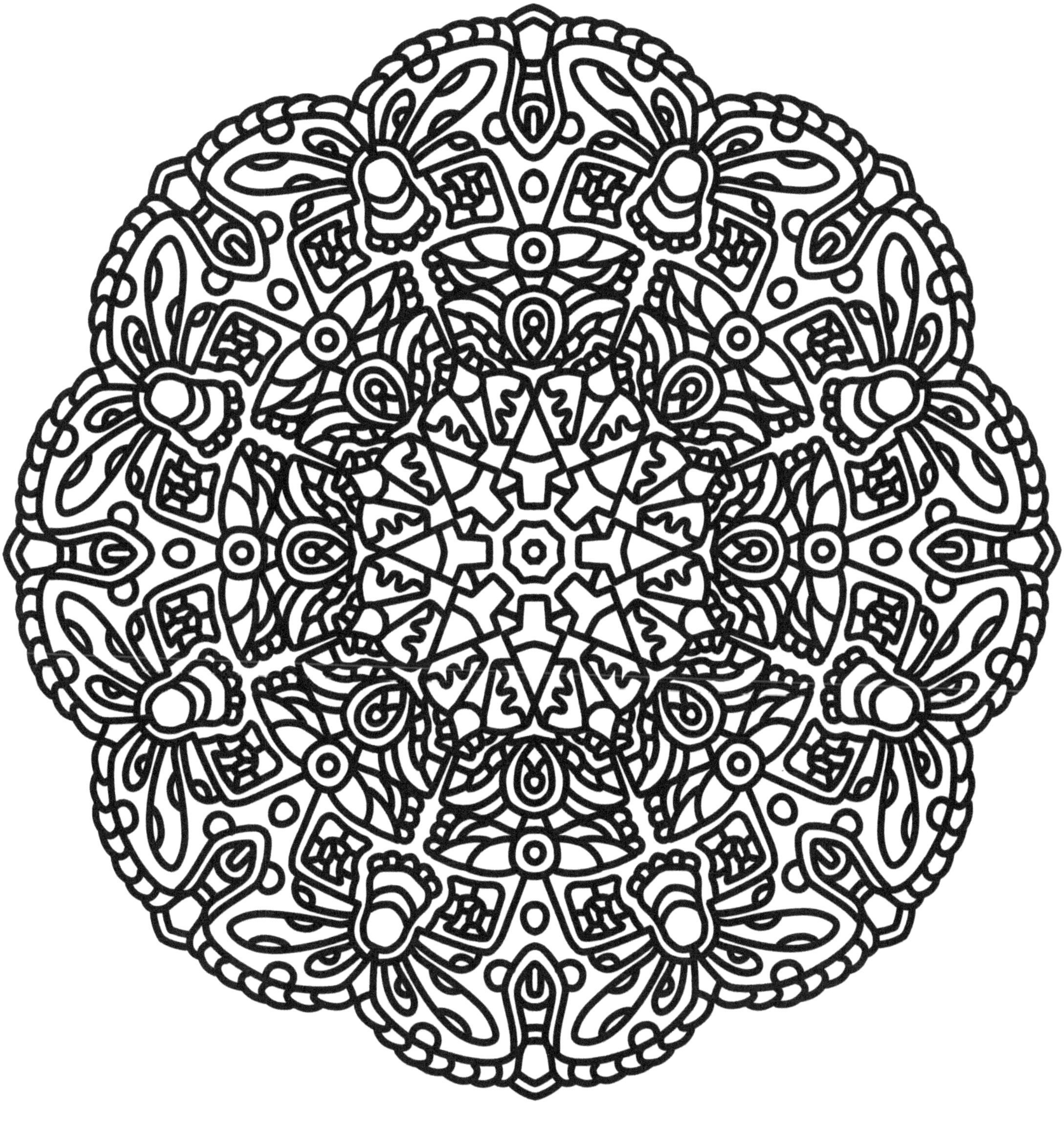

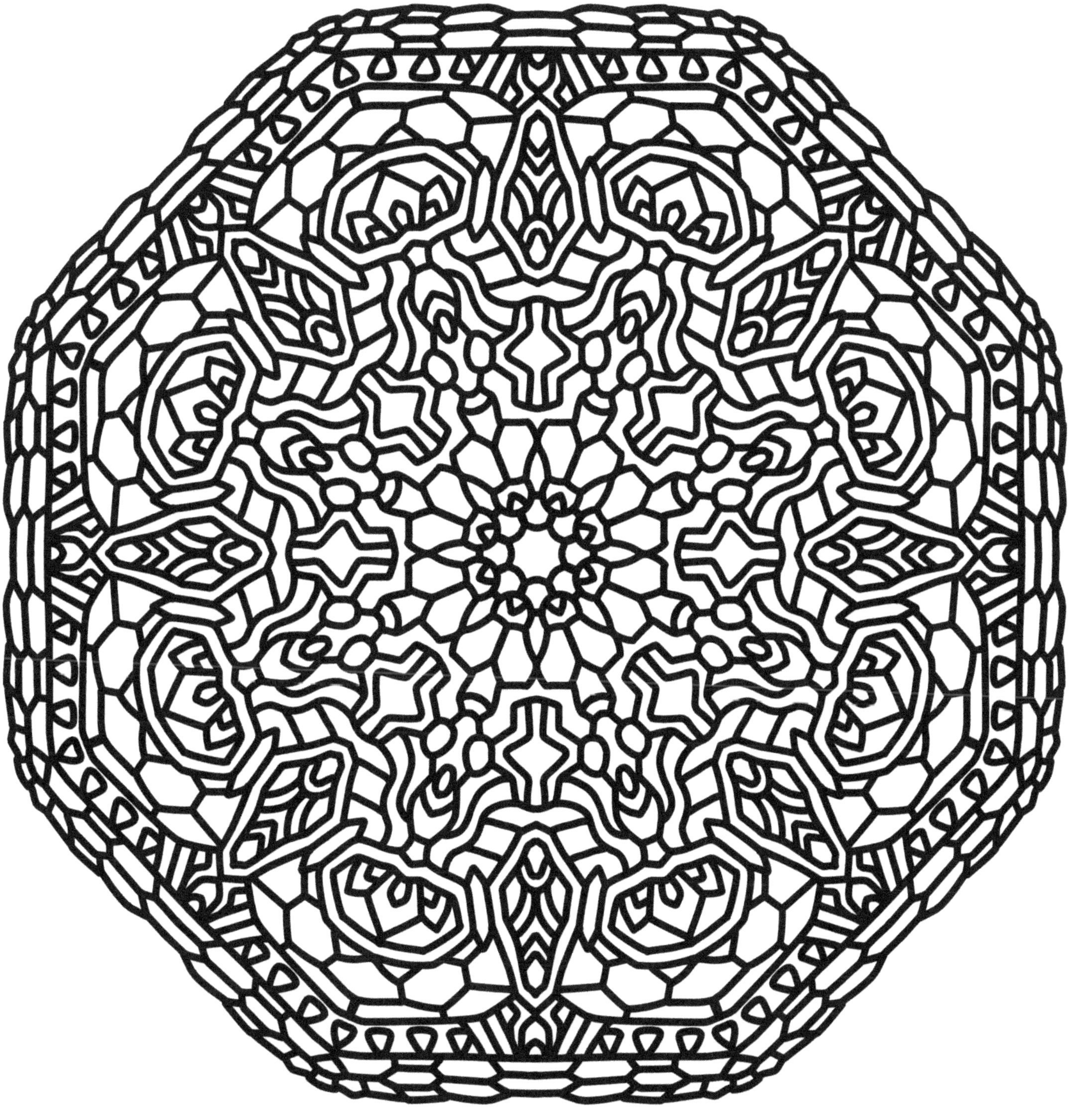

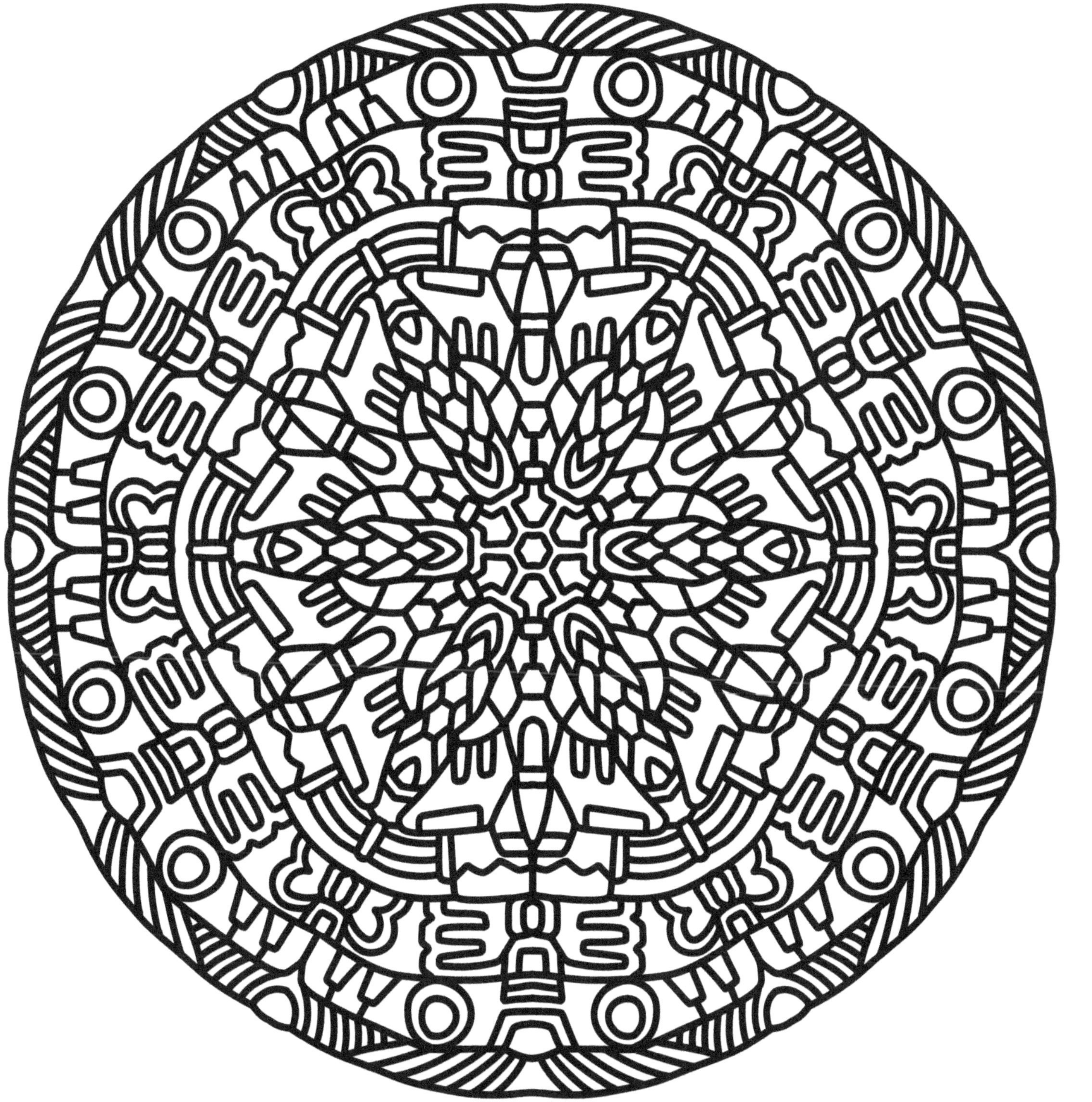

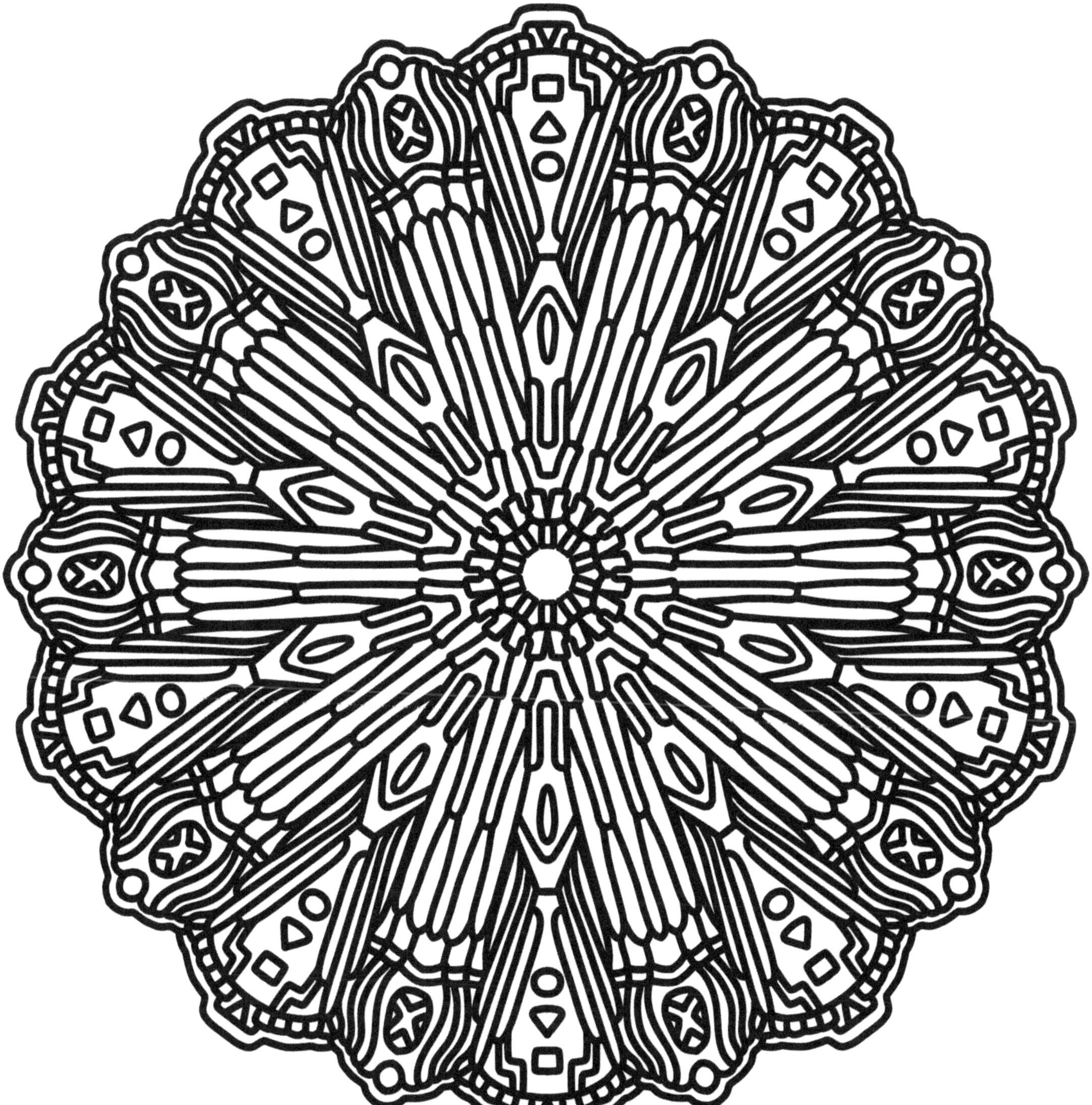

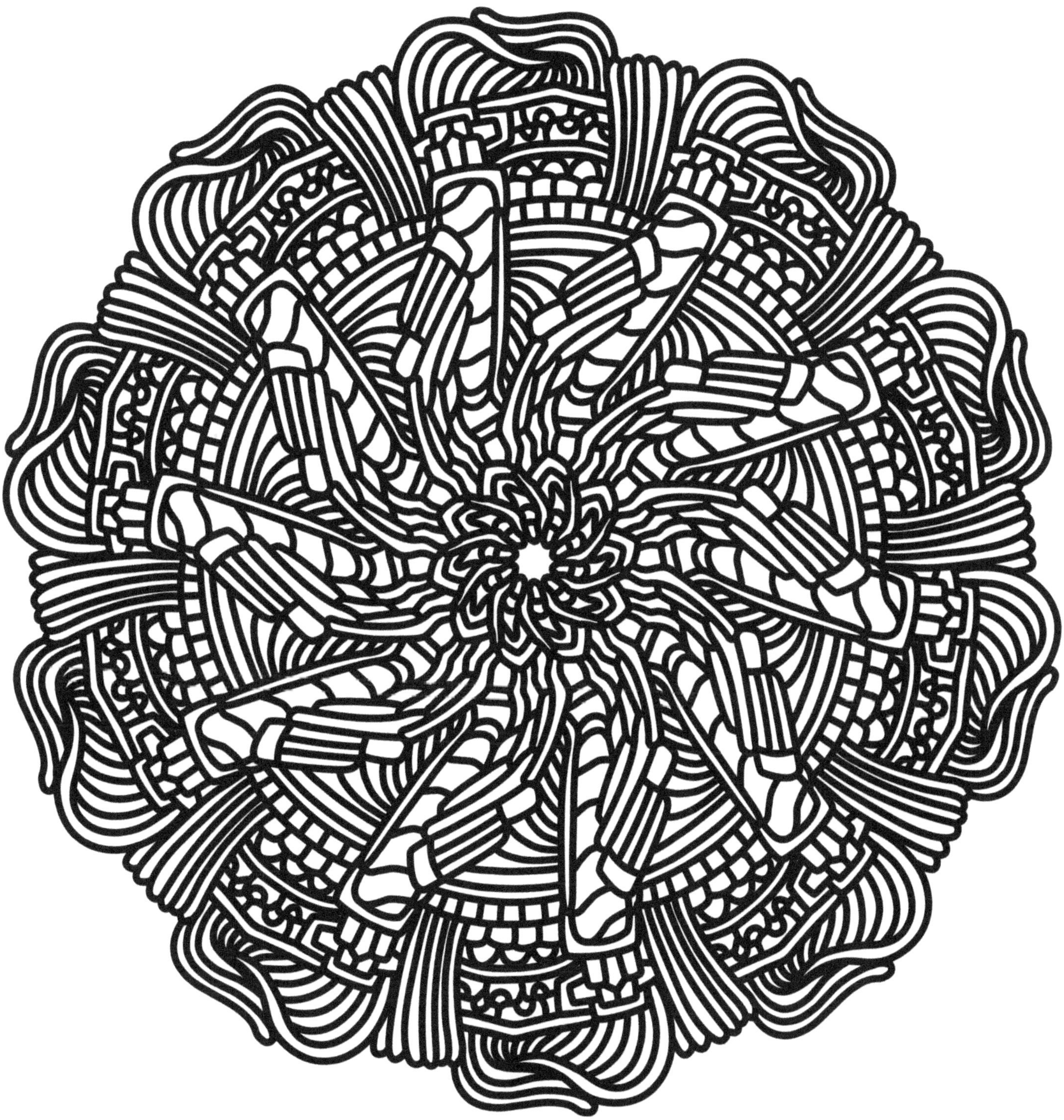

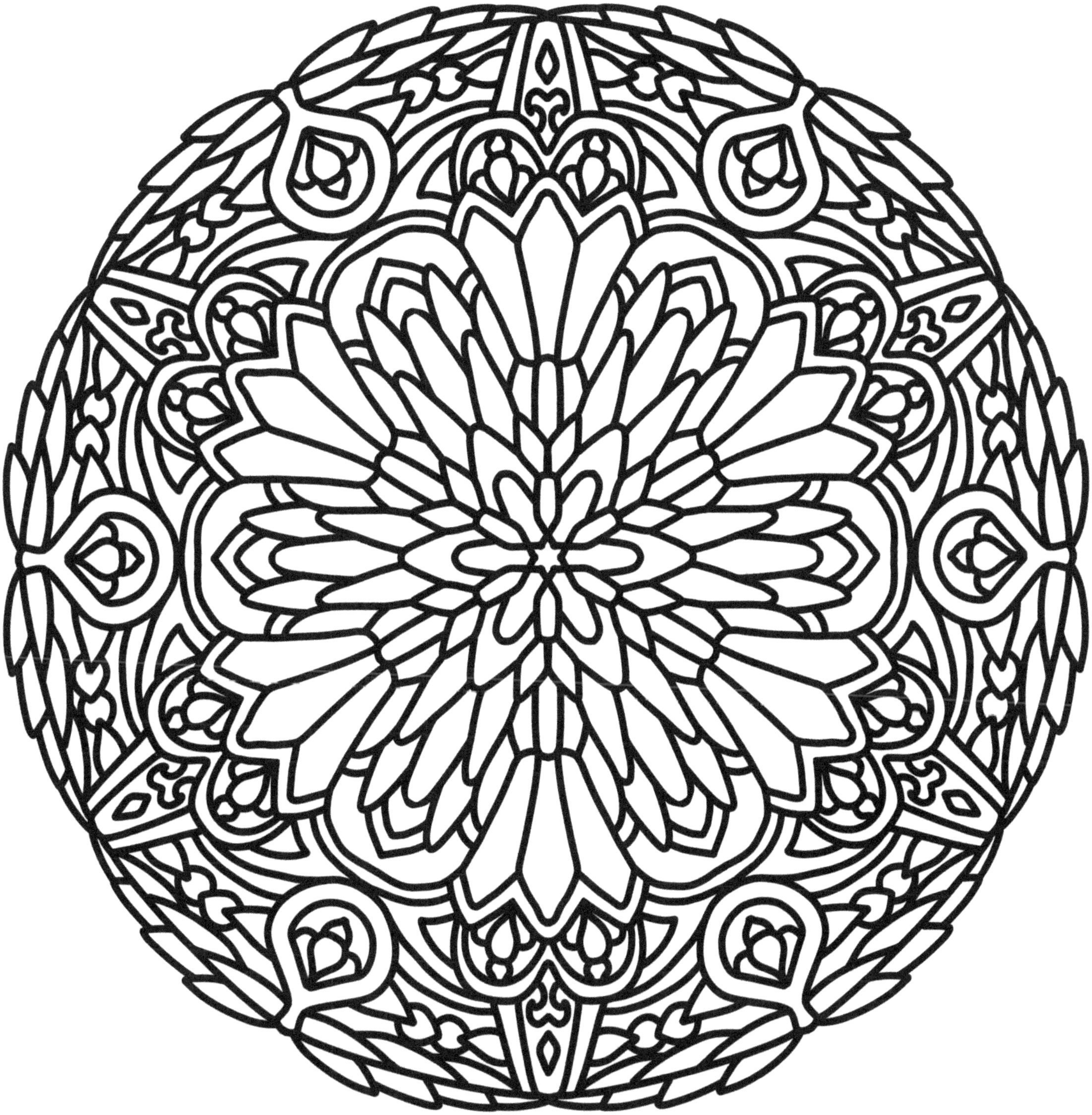

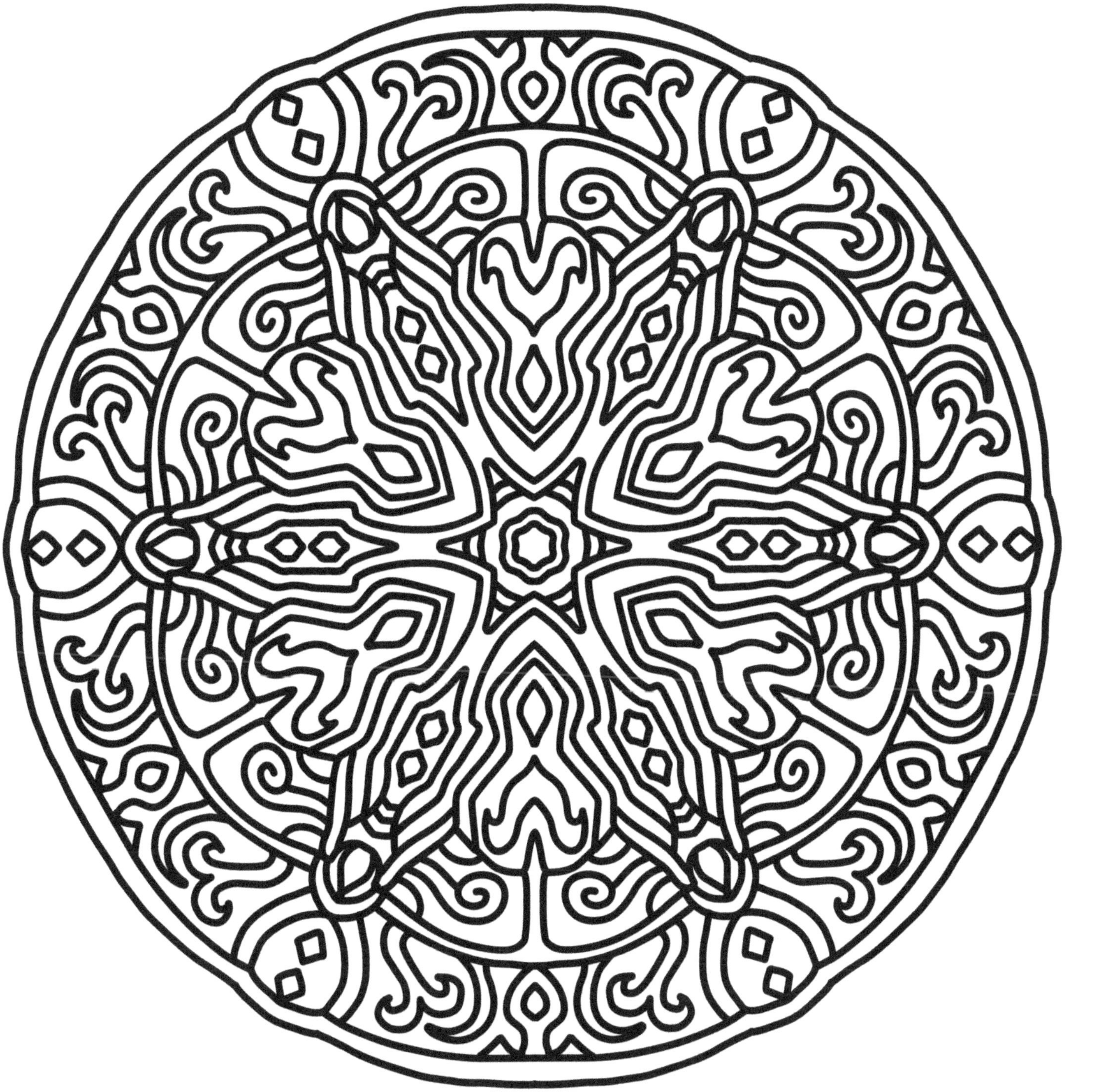

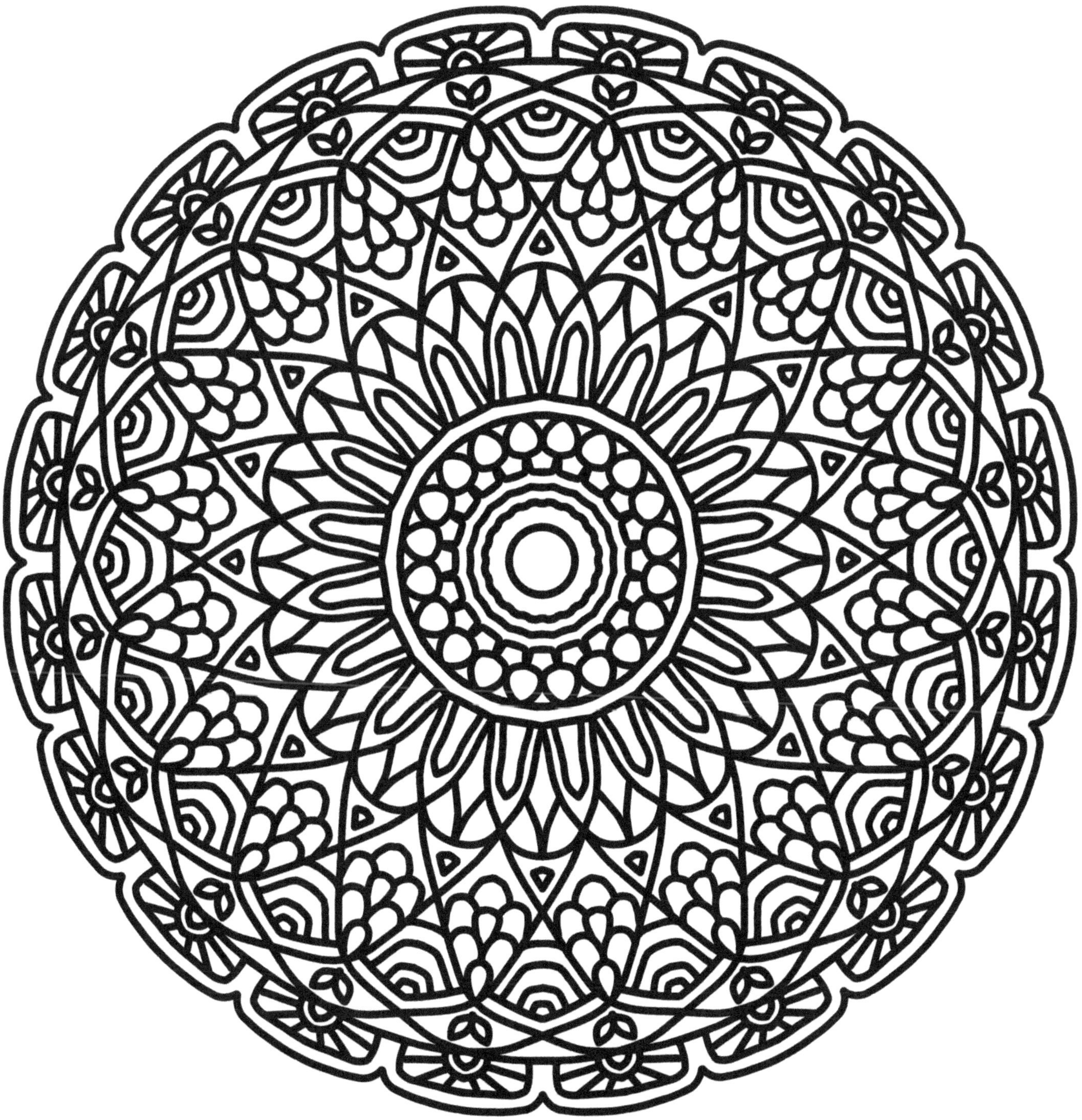

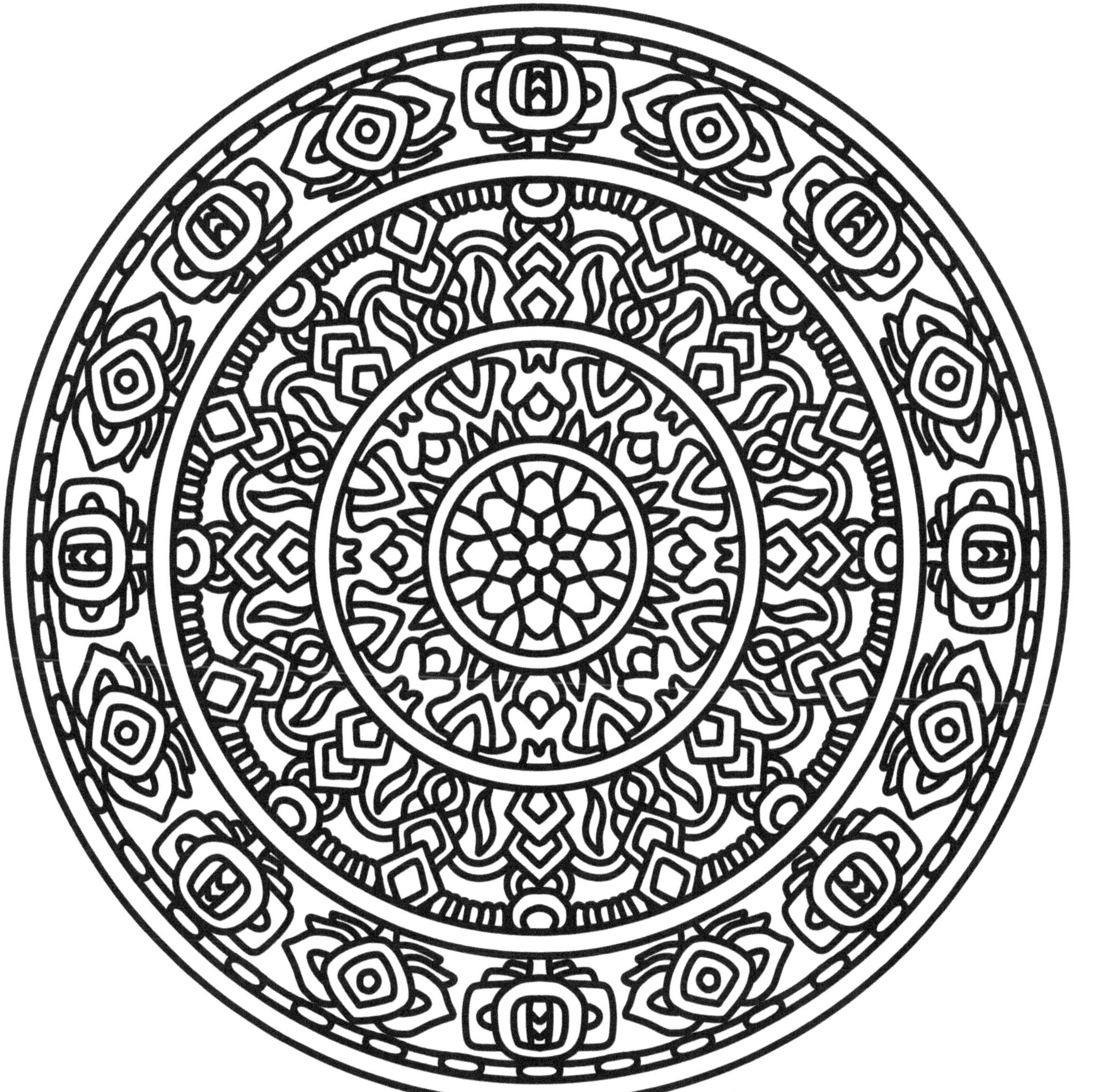

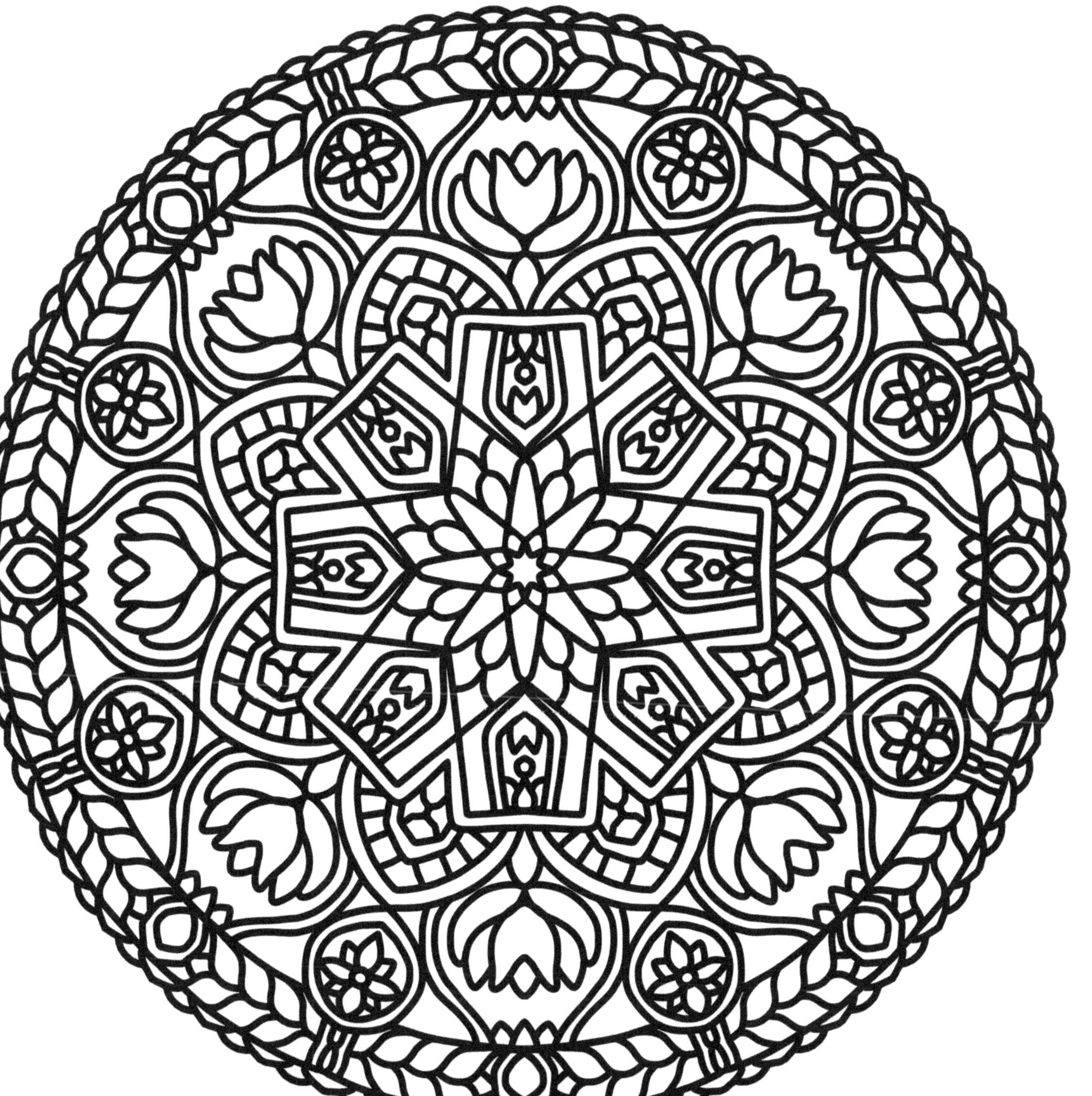

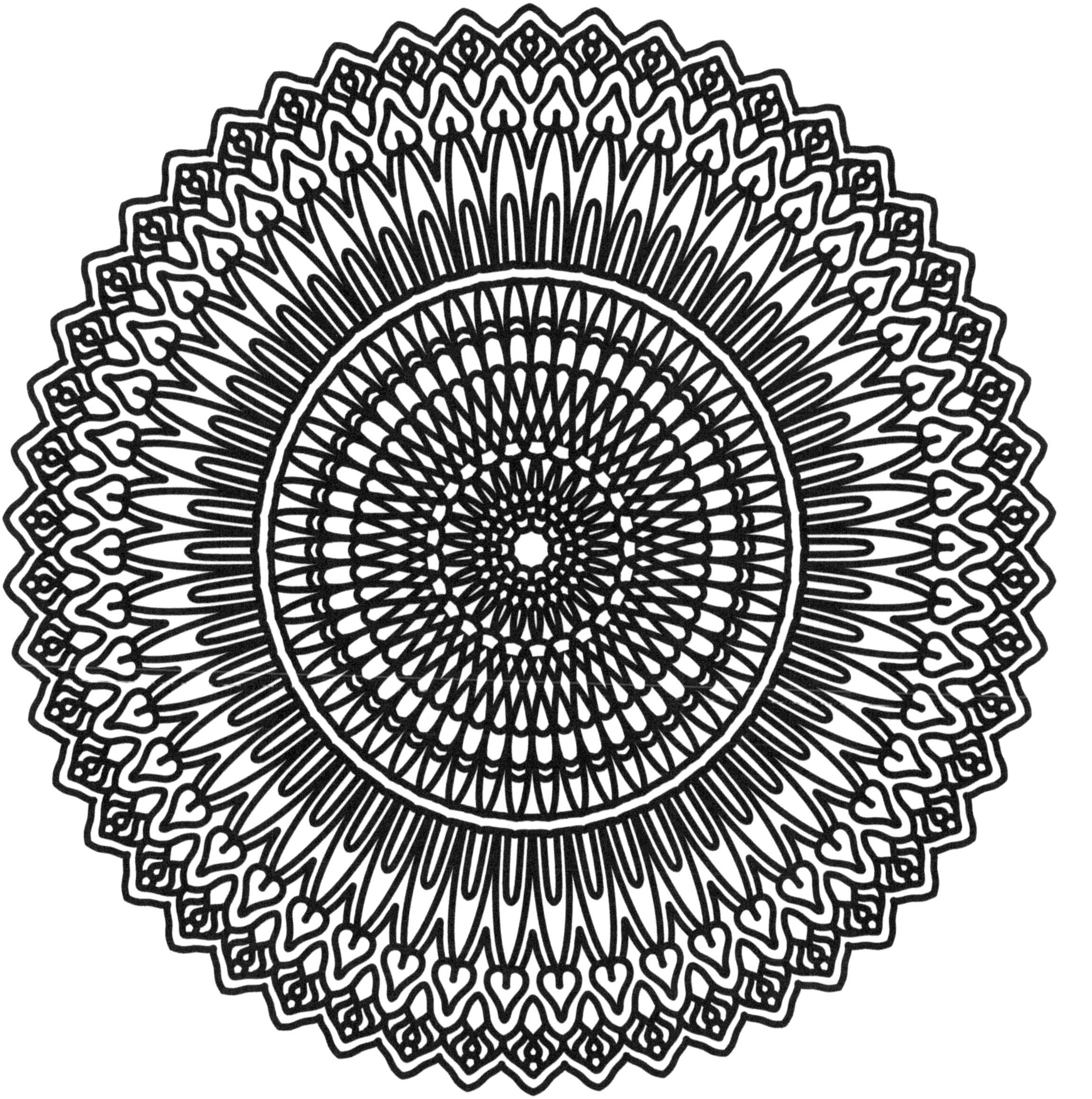

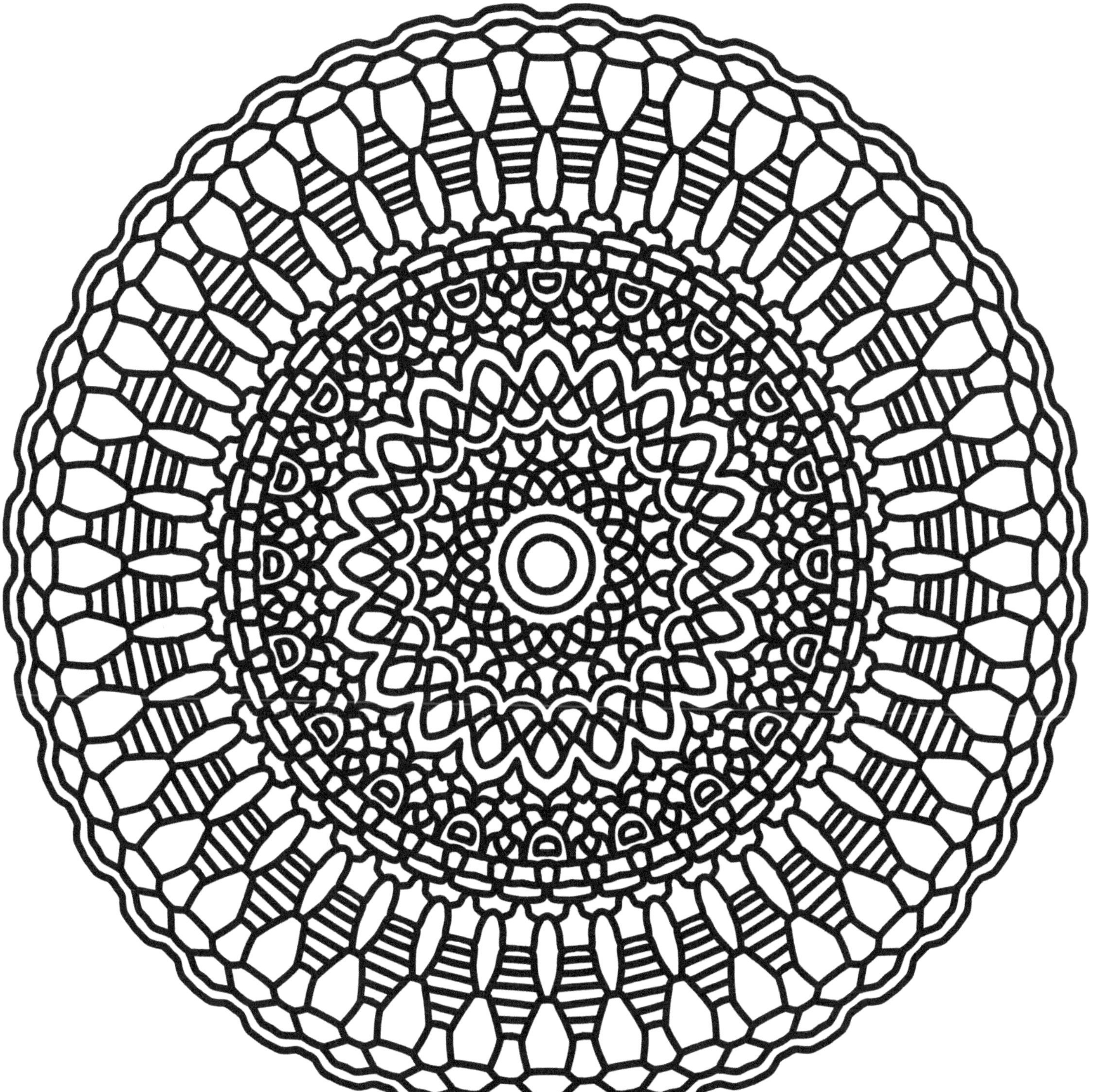

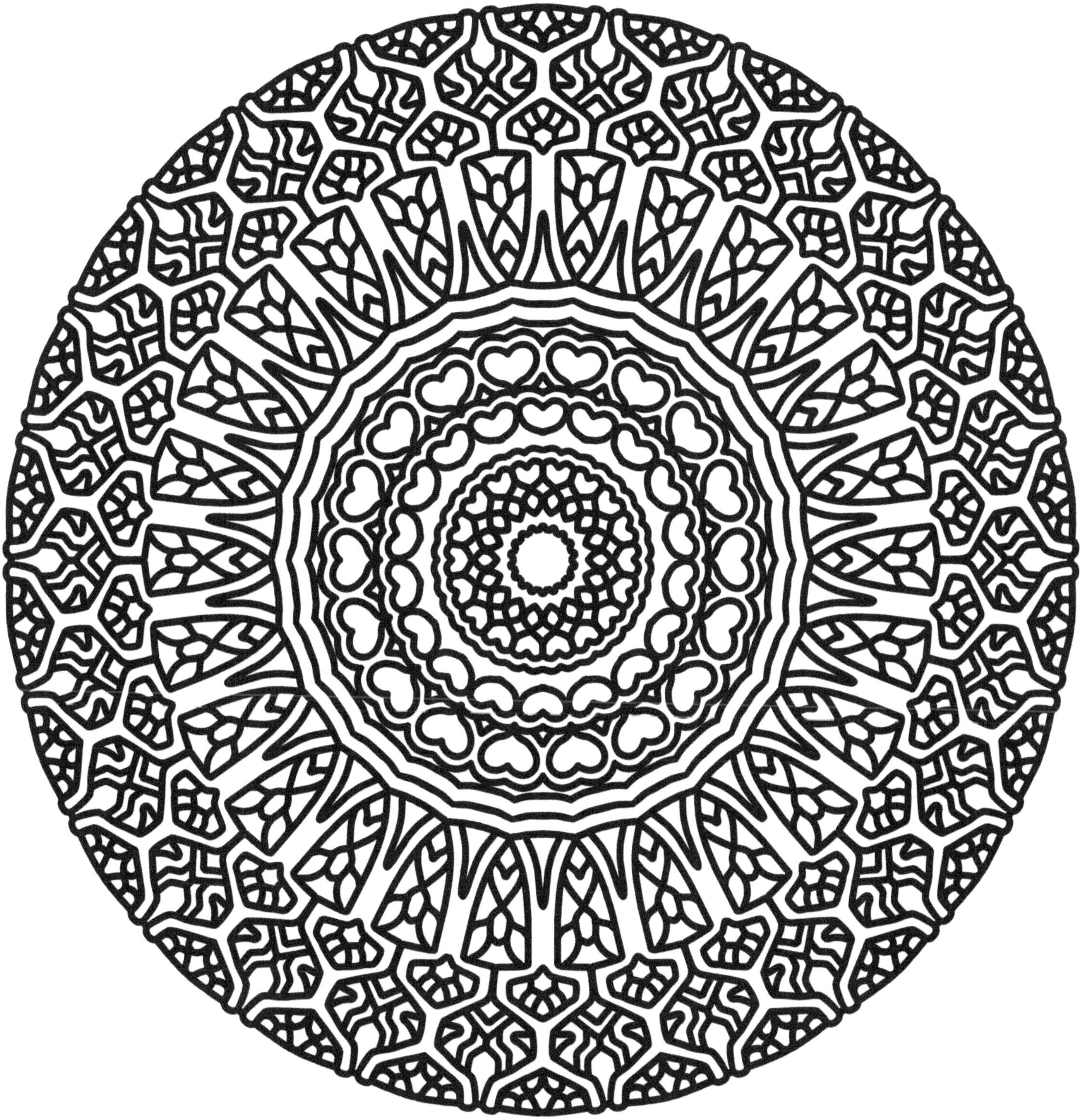

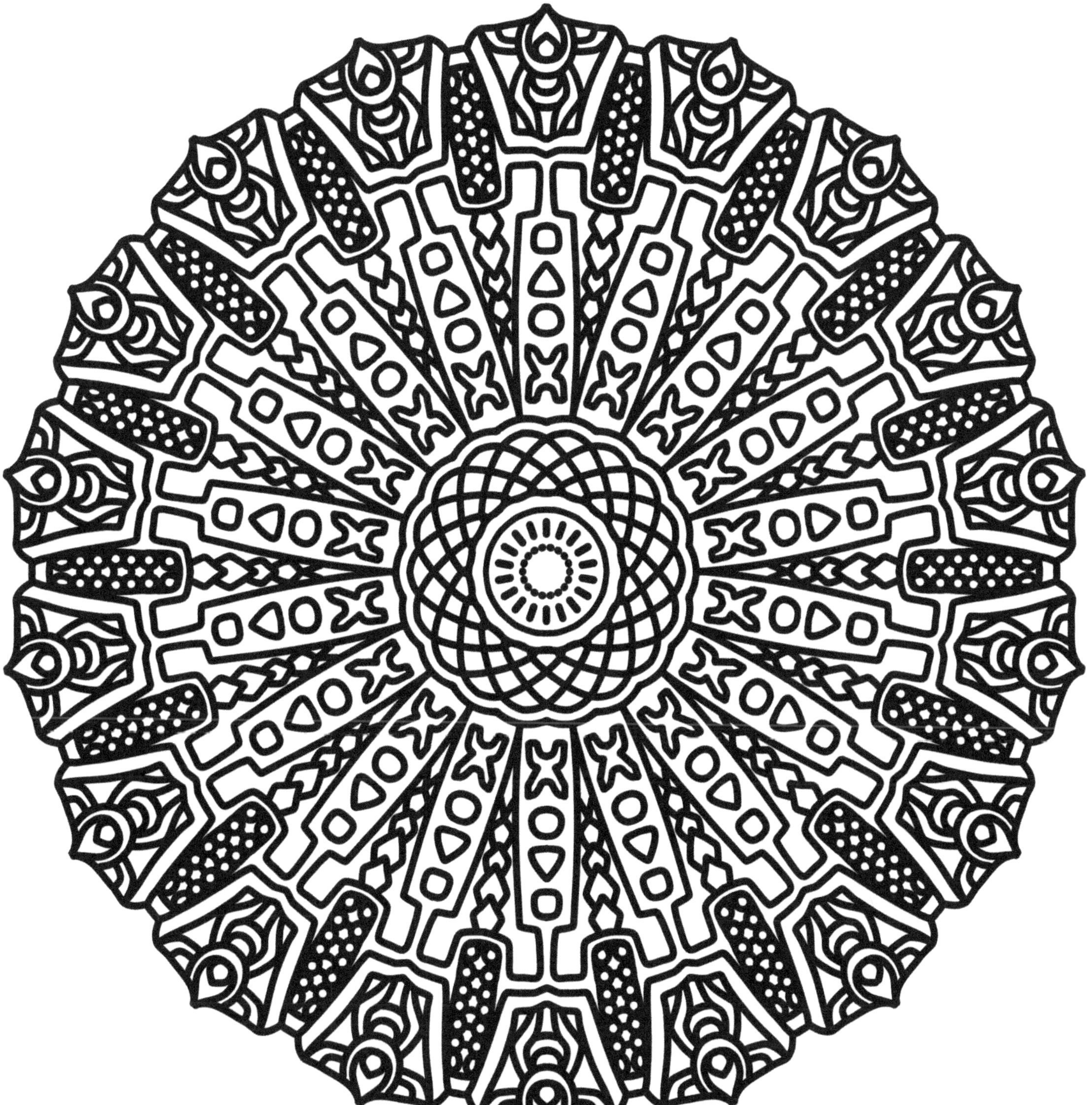

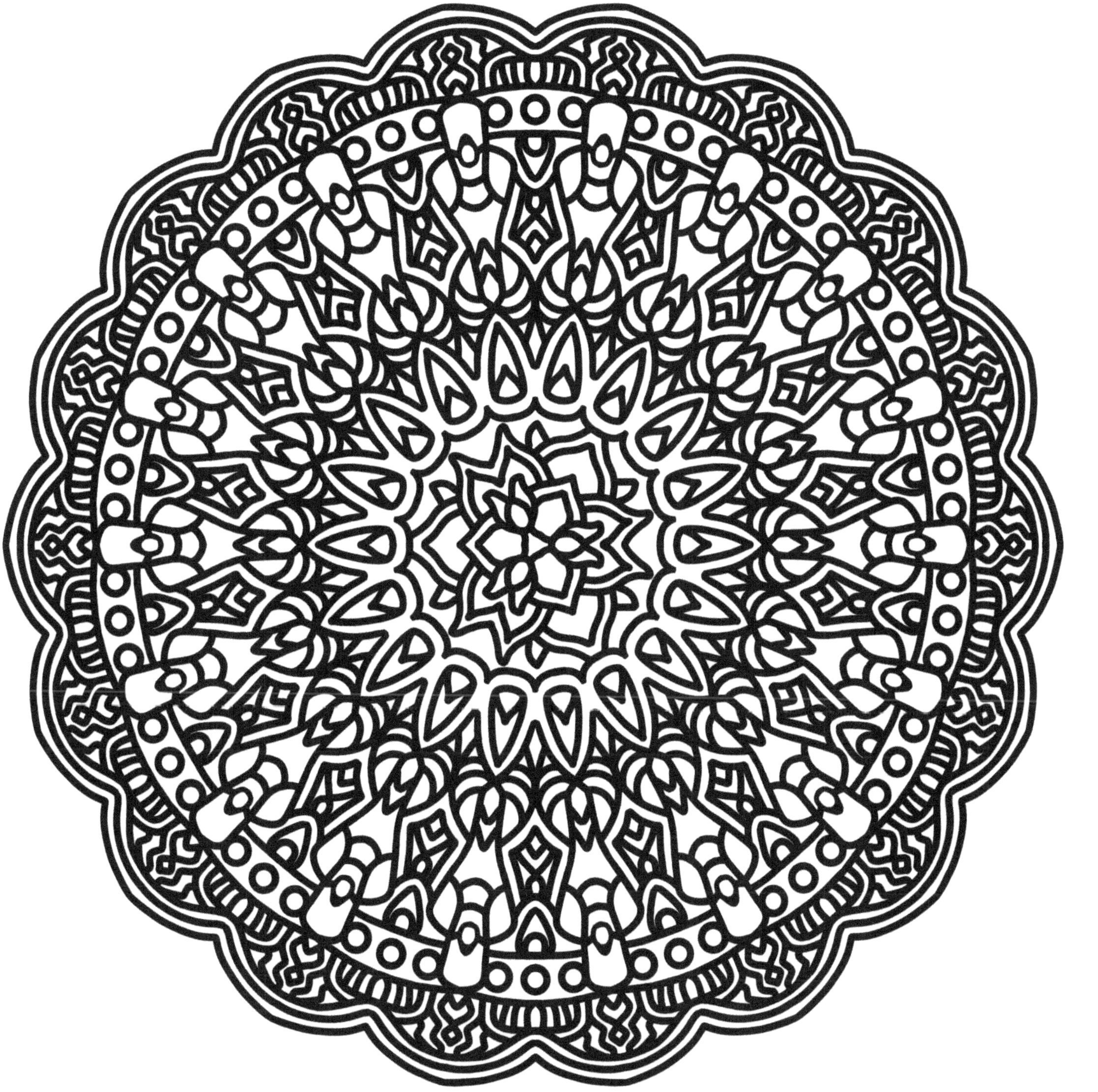

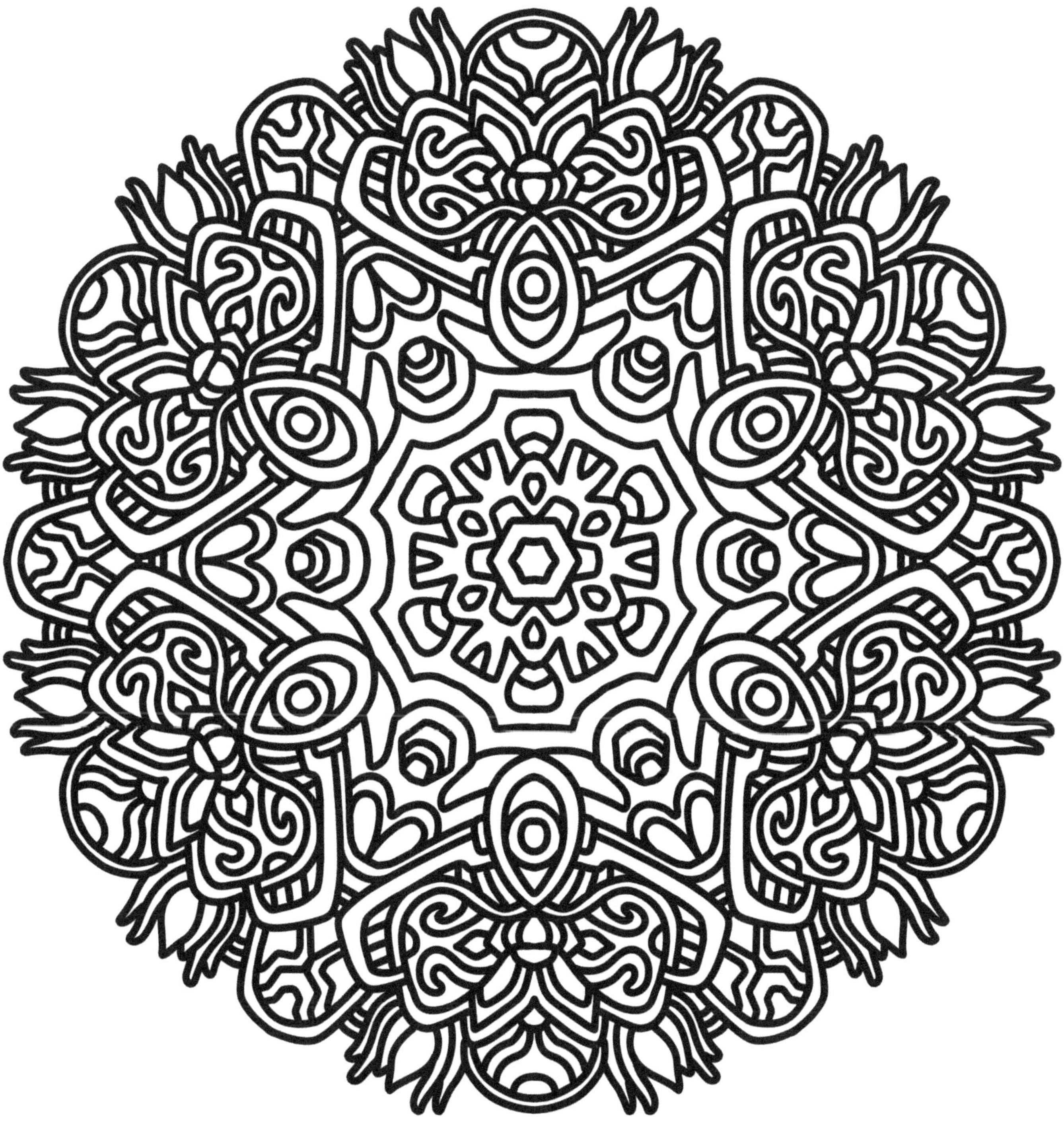

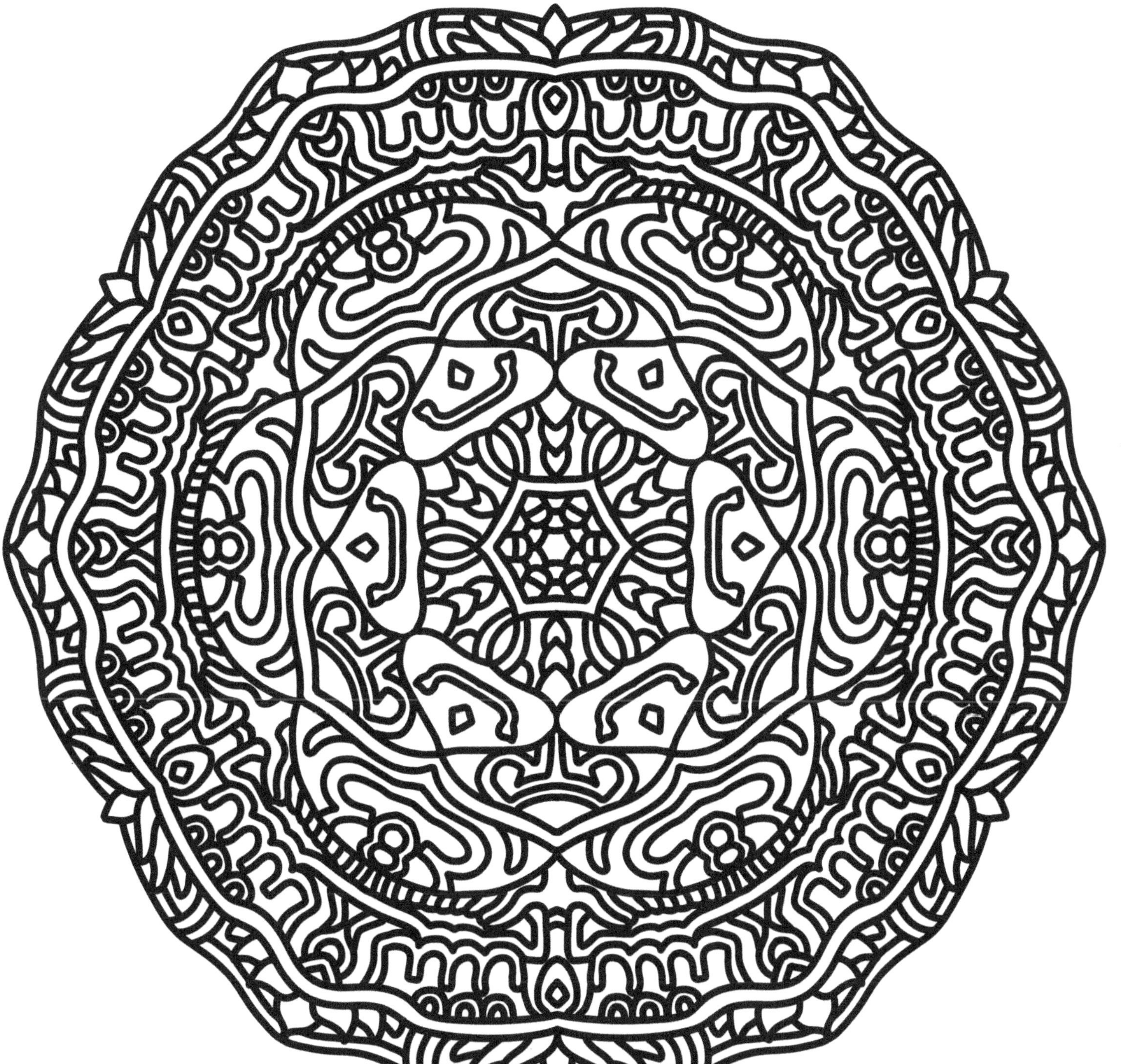

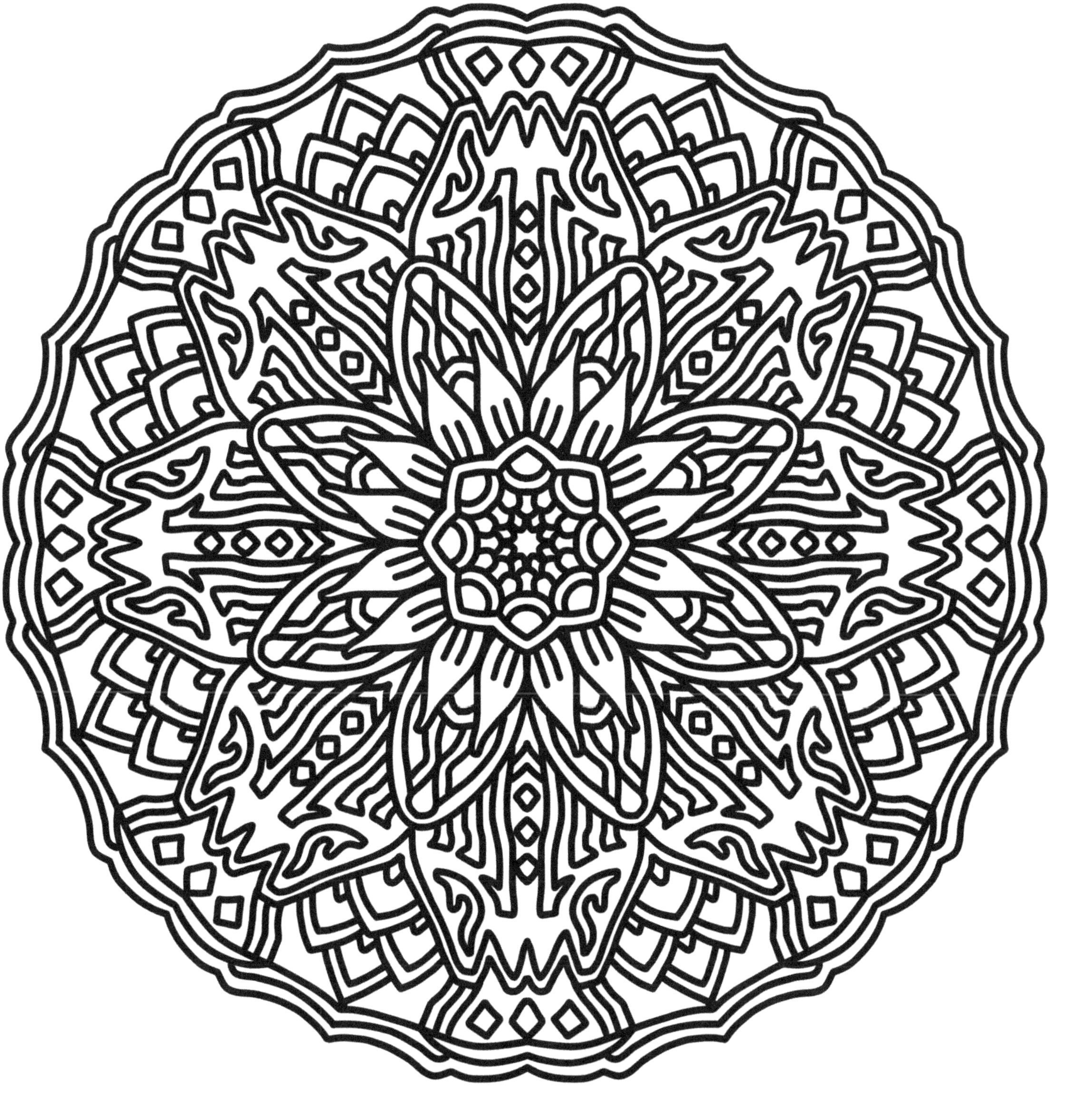

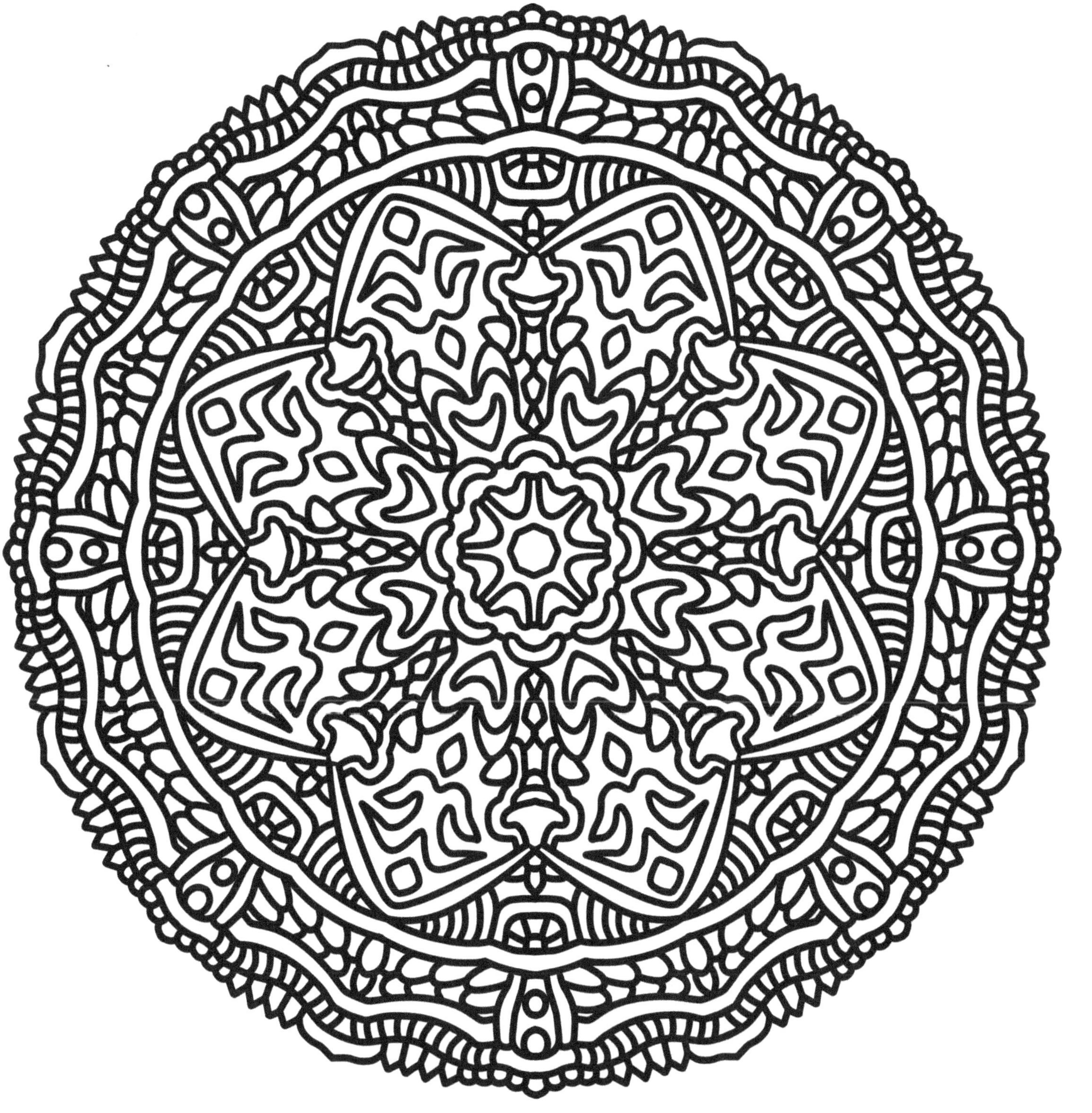

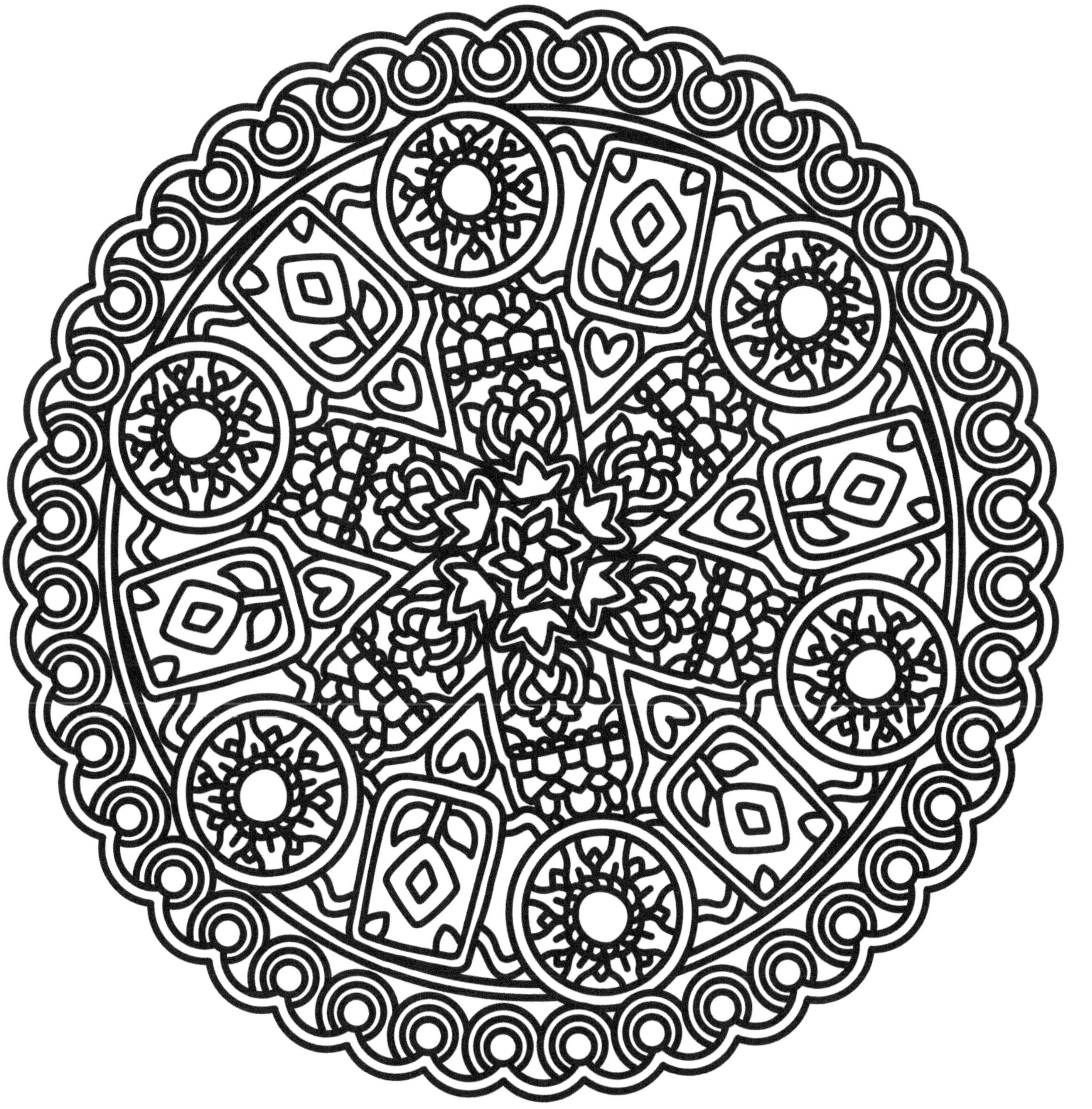

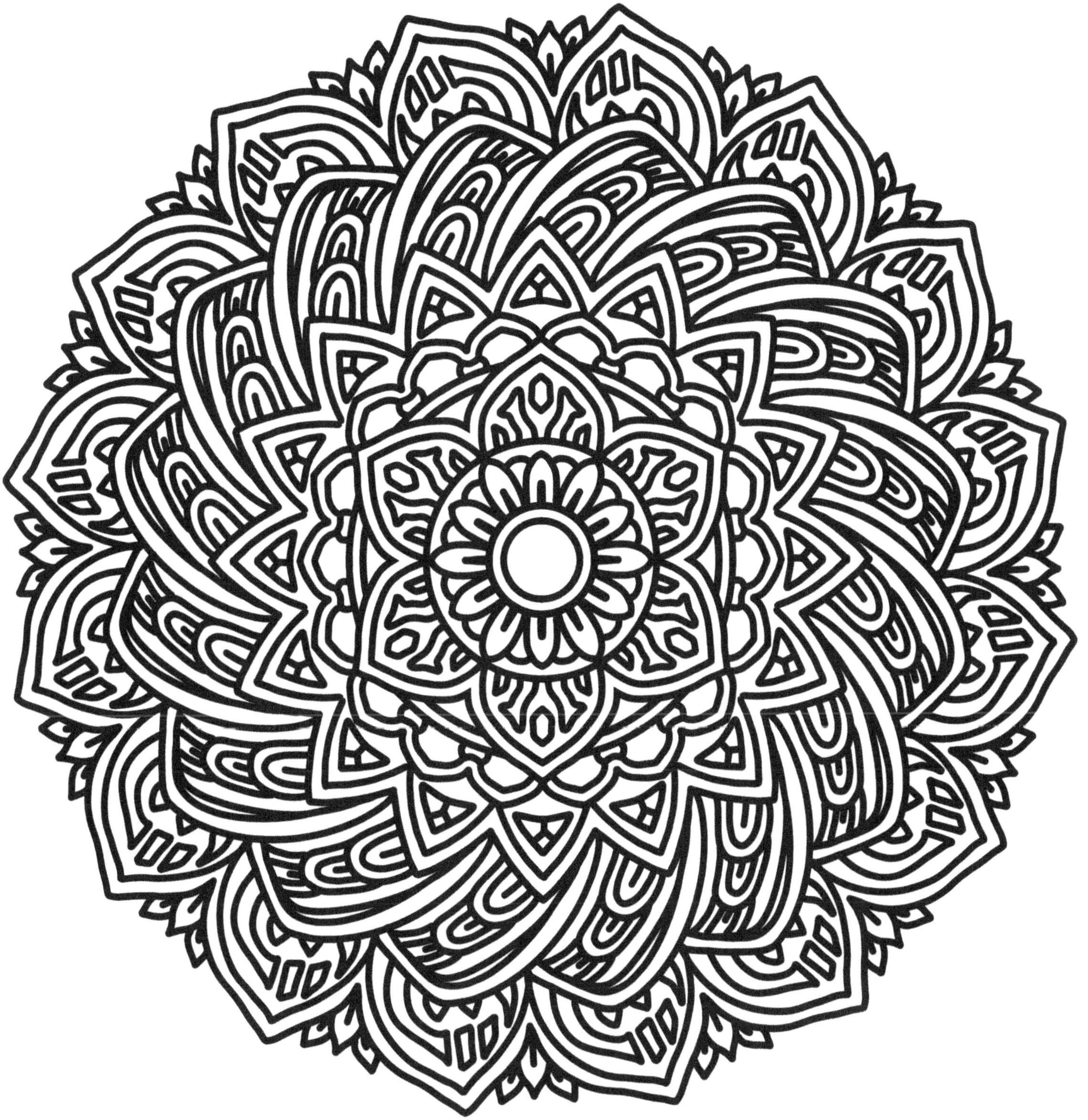

www.ingramcontent.com/pod-product-compliance
Lightning Source LLC
Chambersburg PA
CBHW080650180526
45168CB00008B/3364
* 9 7 8 1 5 1 4 1 9 7 4 5 5 *